Also by Barney Stinson

The Bro Code

BRO
ON THE
GO

BARNEY STINSON
with MATT KUHN

A Touchstone Book
Published by Simon & Schuster
New York   London   Toronto   Sydney

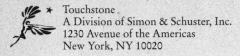

Touchstone
A Division of Simon & Schuster, Inc.
1230 Avenue of the Americas
New York, NY 10020

This Touchstone trade paperback edition November 2009

TOUCHSTONE and colophon are registered trademarks of Simon & Schuster, Inc.

For information about special discounts for bulk purchases, please contact Simon & Schuster Special Sales at 1-866-506-1949 or business@simonandschuster.com.

The Simon & Schuster Speakers Bureau can bring authors to your live event. For more information or to book an event contact the Simon & Schuster Speakers Bureau at 1-866-248-3049 or visit our website at www.simonspeakers.com.

Manufactured in the United States of America

20 19 18 17 16 15 14

Library of Congress Cataloging-in-Publication data is available.

ISBN 978-1-4391-7313-8
ISBN 978-1-4391-7315-2 (ebook)

A portion of this work was published in *The Bro Code* by Touchstone in 2008.

For my vacation home

TABLE OF AWESOME CONTENTS

Contents

INTRODUCTION

FROM THE DISINFECTED DESK
OF BARNEY STINSON

Spider-Man's uncle once said, "With great power comes great responsibility," but what the great philosopher really meant was, "With great power comes a never-ending string of dumbass questions." In the year since selflessly bestowing *The Bro Code* upon humanity I have been inundated with letters, emails, texts—even a few stalker-level break-ins—from people in every corner of the globe, but mostly France.

Everyone wants to know three things:

1. Why haven't you been nominated for a Nobel Prize?
2. How can one person be so handsome, smart, popular, and handsome? (The "one person" I'm referring to is you— Barney Stinson.)
3. *The Bro Code* is immensely entertaining, educational, and

available via Fireside Books/Simon & Schuster, but it offers only general guidelines about how to live my life. What do I do when I'm at the office, going to the beach, or when I'm supposed to be at the office but I'm at the beach? HELP!

I answer:

1. I couldn't possibly nominate myself for *The Bro Code*—they've repeatedly told me it's against the rules—but *you* can.[1] Nominations for the Nobel Prize in Literature are due January 31 and should be addressed to:

Nobel Committee for Literature
Swedish Academy
P.O. Box 2118
SE-103 13 Stockholm
Sweden

---

[1] You being a member of the Swedish Academy or another academy, institution, or society similar to it in construction and purpose; a professor of literature or linguistics at a university or college; or a previous Nobel Prize Laureate in Literature.

2. I don't know, but if you're a hot chick, perhaps we could discuss it at your place sometime . . . though now that I think about it, I probably can't stay very long because I've got a thing later that night—but, yeah, no, let's "talk."

3. Relax. Daddy's home. The next time you're out and about and a Bro-related concern arises, just reach down your pants and whip out this handy reference guide: *Bro on the Go.*

For years I've wanted to supplement the universal laws of the Bro Code with a portable handbook of advice and commentary but for various reasons had to scuttle each previous effort: *The Guy-dance Counselor,*[1] *Touching Your Inner Bro,*[2] and most recently *The Pocket Stinson.*[3] Now, with *Bro on the Go,* I'm finally able to present the observations, reflective wisdom, and inspirational nuggets I've mined through the daily grind of being awesome.

---

[1] Sold title rights to adult film industry

[2] Sold title rights to adult film industry

[3] Sold title rights and life story to adult film industry—in negotiations to star in the movie or at least "pitch in" on casting decisions

In these pages you will find official Bro Codes in bold print alongside my own unique and powerful insights. To maximize utility, I've organized this volume by location so that a Bro trying to choose between black or gray spandex shorts for his workout can quickly flip to "A Bro at the Gym" and know the answer is a resounding "neither." Used this way, it is my hope that *The Bro Code* will calibrate your moral compass while *Bro on the Go* provides a map to navigate your path toward total awesomeness and maybe, just maybe, getting laid big-time.

With these tools in hand (heh), you are now armed to live the life of a Bro on the Go. So take this package of wisdom, roll it into a generous cylinder, stuff it in your front pocket, and go, Bro, go.

A Bro
on a Date

A Bro is under no obligation to open a door for anyone. If women insist on having their own professional basketball league, then they can open their own doors. Honestly, they're not that heavy.

Good word to say a lot on a first date?
"Trustworthy."

Bad word to say a lot on a first date?
"Mommy."

Manners dictate that you wait
for your date to go to the restroom
before checking out whether
that blonde in the corner is indeed
spank material.

Sure, the popcorn trick sounds like
a great idea, but nobody's actually ever
done it. And that's why she'll
never see it coming.

You can learn a lot about someone
on a first date, but the only way to get
her weight is to steal her driver's license.

A Bro
Behind
the Wheel

A Bro never admits he can't drive stick. Even after an accident.

This is all the car in front of you's fault.

That whole "sexy female cop with handcuffs and whipped cream" thing happens far less than the adult film industry would lead you to believe.

Remember when you paid extra
because you had to have a sunroof?

At a four-way stop, "Bros before ho's" still applies.

(Heh. "Four-way.")

Jumping through the window
Dukes of Hazzard style is fun.
Landing with the emergency break
between your legs isn't.

A Bro
in His Pad

If a Bro gets a dog, it must be at least as tall as his knee when full-grown.

An adult channel home is
a happy home.

Stuffing your matching sheet sets inside one of the pillowcases is a no-fuss way to keep your linens organized.

Even if it means banging a pot
during battle scenes, a Bro
should make some sort of attempt
at surround sound.

A Bro
at the
Movies

If two Bros decide to catch a movie together, they may not attend a screening that begins after 4:40 P.M. Also, despite the cost savings, they shall not split a tub of popcorn, choosing instead to procure individual bags.

If it looks like you'll be staring at
a giant Gwyneth Paltrow, Sandra
Bullock, or Dame Judi Dench
for the next ninety minutes, remember:
Die Hard is probably on TV right now.

Appropriate seating arrangement
for two Bros:

Bro — [empty "we're just Bros" seat] — Bro.

Just a hunch, but I bet
the vice president/general/police chief
from the beginning is somehow
behind all this.

No matter how bad it is,
DO NOT WALK OUT OF
A KATE WINSLET FILM:
83 percent chance of a rack cameo,
highest of any multiple
Academy Award nominee.

A Bro
at the
Strip Club

In a scenario where two or more Bros are watching entertainment of the adult variety, one Bro is forbidden from intentionally or unintentionally touching another Bro in ANY capacity.

This is not the venue to try out
that new black light.

There are a million reasons not to use a credit card here, but only two silicone-filled reasons why you probably will.

A fun trick to play is to tell
that 6 foot 8 bouncer
that your Bro is groping all the girls.

Some handy Russian phrases:

"Good evening."

"Boy, it sure is nice to unwind after
a long day at the immigration office."

"As a matter of fact, I've got a whole
box of blank green cards back
at my apartment."

A Bro
at the
Game

When wearing a baseball cap, a Bro may position the brim at either 12 or 6 o'clock. All other angles are reserved for rappers and the handicapped.

When Bros attend a sporting event
and see themselves on the
JumboTron, they shall purse
their lips and flex their biceps
while informing the crowd that
their team is number one, despite any
objective rankings to the contrary.

Even though you're in the upper deck and he's on the mound, yes, the pitcher can hear you shouting. More to the point, he'll never know that giving up that two-run homer has pretty much blown the team's chances of victory unless you personally tell him so.

The stranger sitting next to you would totally like to hear about your high school sports moment of glory.

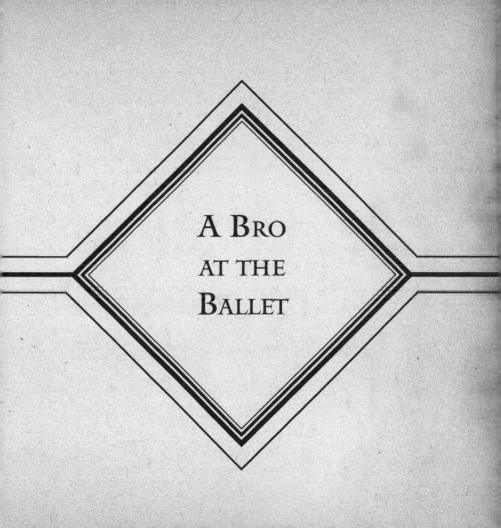

A BRO
AT THE
BALLET

n/a

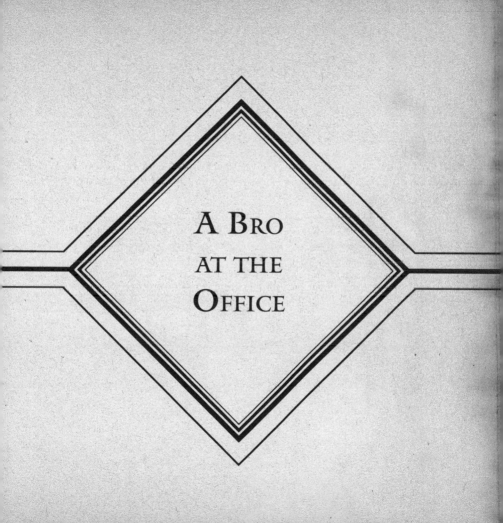

A Bro
at the
Office

A Bro shall never mix it up
romantically with a co-worker.[1]

---

[1] EXCEPTIONS: Co-worker is an eight or better; you are co-worker's superior; co-worker dresses a little slutty; getting fired from job not such a bad thing; company recently sued for sexual harassment—unlikely to happen again; someone makes a bet that you can't; you are switching floors soon; you and co-worker get stuck in an elevator; you hit the emergency button and get "stuck" in the elevator with co-worker; co-worker going to be fired, or soon will be, after you sabotage co-worker's files; you mixed it up with co-worker before becoming co-workers; co-worker hits on you; you are in a little bit of a rut, romantically speaking; co-worker going through divorce; co-worker looking pretty good lately; co-worker not offended when you "accidentally" email provocative pictures of self to office.

As collegial as your office might be, nobody wants to see you exit the restroom and announce, "I just dropped a bomb in there."

"Had trouble sleeping last night" is
a crude but time-tested cover
for a bad hangover.

If you're giving a presentation and
your mind suddenly goes blank,
you can always start chanting
"U-S-A! U-S-A!"

"Clear browser history" saves jobs.

A Bro
at the
Mall

A Bro doesn't comparison shop.

Don't look back—they were
definitely teenagers.

There's always time for a casual lap around the electronics superstore.

Lingering around the children's play area to scope out the hot young moms is a good idea in theory only.

A Bro
on a
Bro'd Trip

If a scenario arises in which a Bro has promised two of his Bros permanent shotgun, one of the following shall determine the copilot: (1) foot race to the car, (2) silent auction, or in the case of a road trip exceeding 450 miles, (3) a no-holds-barred cage match to the death.

A considerate Bro rolls down the window before dropping ass in the car.

When I say "Doritos," I mean *Cool Ranch* Doritos. Remember that at the rest stop 'cause I'm just gonna send you back in there.

If you find yourselves in Montana,
somebody screwed up somewhere.

A Bro
at a
Dance Club

A Bro never dances with his hands over his head.

Two Bros shall maintain at least
a three-foot radius between them
while dancing on the same floor,
even when reenacting the knife fight
from "Beat It," which, I guess,
two Bros shouldn't do anyway,
or at least not very often.

Don't be "necklace guy."

FREAKIN' LOUD IN HERE, HUH?

A Bro
at the
Gym

A Bro shall not lollygag if he must get naked in front of other Bros in a gym locker room.

Judge not the Bro who asks a chick
to spot him on the bench press.

Judge the Bro who does so
with an erection.

God did not design spandex for dudes.

Exception: David Lee Roth in the '80s. That just *worked*.

Injuring yourself trying to lift
more weight than the next guy
proves nothing . . . except how
awesome you are.

Surprise! You're not the only guy
who joined this step class
to meet chicks.

Briefs before boxers.

The leg press is designed to showcase the calves, hamstrings, and quadriceps, not your dimpled scrotum.

Be nice to every woman in the gym because, as the old saying goes:

"Today's heavy chick is tomorrow's hot chick."

NOTE: Unless their face is dingo city, in which case feel free to act however you please.

If your plan is to hang out in the sauna
until someone other than a fat Eastern
European man steps in, then, buddy,
I hope you like heat stroke.

A Bro
at a
Renaissance
Faire

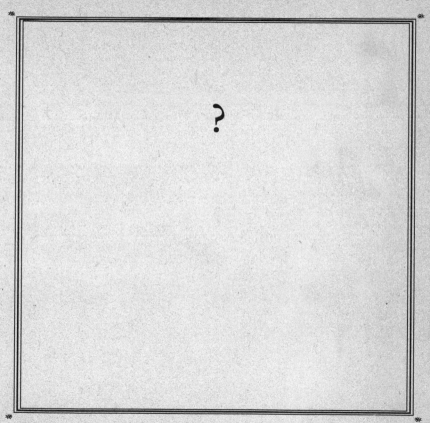

A Bro
at the
Beach

A Bro never wears socks with sandals.
He commits to one cohesive
footgear plan and sticks with it.

A "clothing optional" beach doesn't really mean "clothing optional" for Bros.

People are afraid of sharks, but in many
ways aren't they just the Bros
of the ocean?

A watched bikini top never
malfunctions.

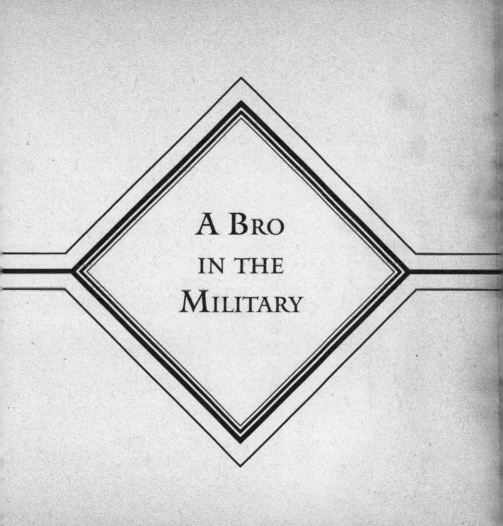

A BRO
IN THE
MILITARY

A Bro loves his country, unless that country isn't America.

If some smug citizen reminds you that
he paid for your education, it's okay
to demonstrate your acquired
knowledge by kicking him
in the nuts.

"Don't ask, don't tell" also refers to farts.

If you're in New York City for Fleet Week and you happen to see me chatting up some honey in my rented sailor uniform, let's maybe keep it between us, 'kay?

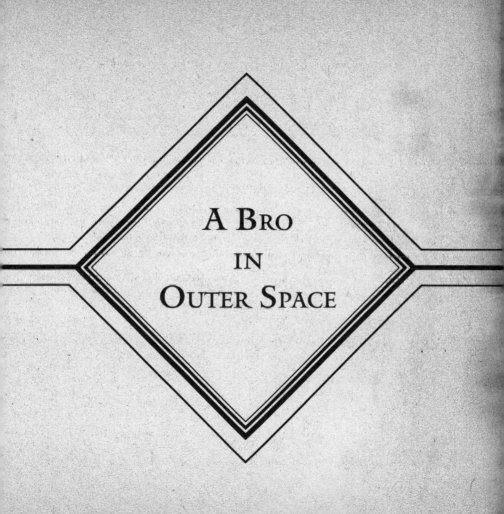

A Bro
in
Outer Space

In a gravity-free environment, one Bro
isn't always expected to Bro out
another Bro by letting said Bro go first.
For example, if the former Bro had
the chance to be the First Bro
on the Moon but was like,
"No, go ahead Bro, it's all you."
That's just stupid, Bro.

Stay alert.

Sometimes your onboard computer is
your robot Bro. Other times
he will try to kill you.

Ast-BRO-naut.

Right? Right?!

A Bro
in the
Bathroom

Even in a drought, a Bro flushes twice.

An hour spent sculpting a neck beard
is an hour lost forever.

You'll know you've found your "bathroom read" when your legs fall asleep.

It'd be a much more sanitary world
if they made soap shaped like boobs.

NOTE: Don't steal my boob-shaped-soap idea. I'm gonna
do something with that.

A Bro
at a
Party

A Bro shows up at another Bro's party with at least one more unit of alcohol than he plans to drink. If the party sucks and/or there are too many dudes, the Bro is entitled to leave with his alcohol, though etiquette dictates he should wait until nobody is looking.

Remain calm, walk away slowly,
and nobody will know you broke that.

If you're working on a chick and she mentions her cat more than three times, cut your losses and get out of there.

A Bro
at the
Bar

Given an option on quantity
when ordering a beer with his Bros,
a Bro always selects the largest size
available or shall never hear the end
of it that night.

If you opened a bar, it would be
way cooler than this.

No matter how much you tip her, that hot bartender just ain't gonna happen.

If you really like a bar, don't be there when the lights come on after last call.

You will never return.

If you can read this, you're far too sober
for darts, karaoke, and that woman
in the corner whose eyebrows are
high-fiving in the middle.

A Bro
with His
Fiancée at a Thai
Cooking
Class

Seriously?

ABOUT BARNEY,
BY BARNEY

BARNEY STINSON is a handsome man you can totally trust your daughters with who is best known for blowing up the blogosphere with www.barneysblog.com and for sleeping with more than 200 women. Barney speaks 83 different languages, can move small objects with his mind, is a professional athlete,[1] and may or may not be involved in the sexy world of espionage. Oh, and every year he builds orphanages or wells or whatever in poor areas of the world, if that's the sort of thing that turns you on.

---

[1] The Professional Laser Tag Association (PLTA) is awaiting both funding and general interest.